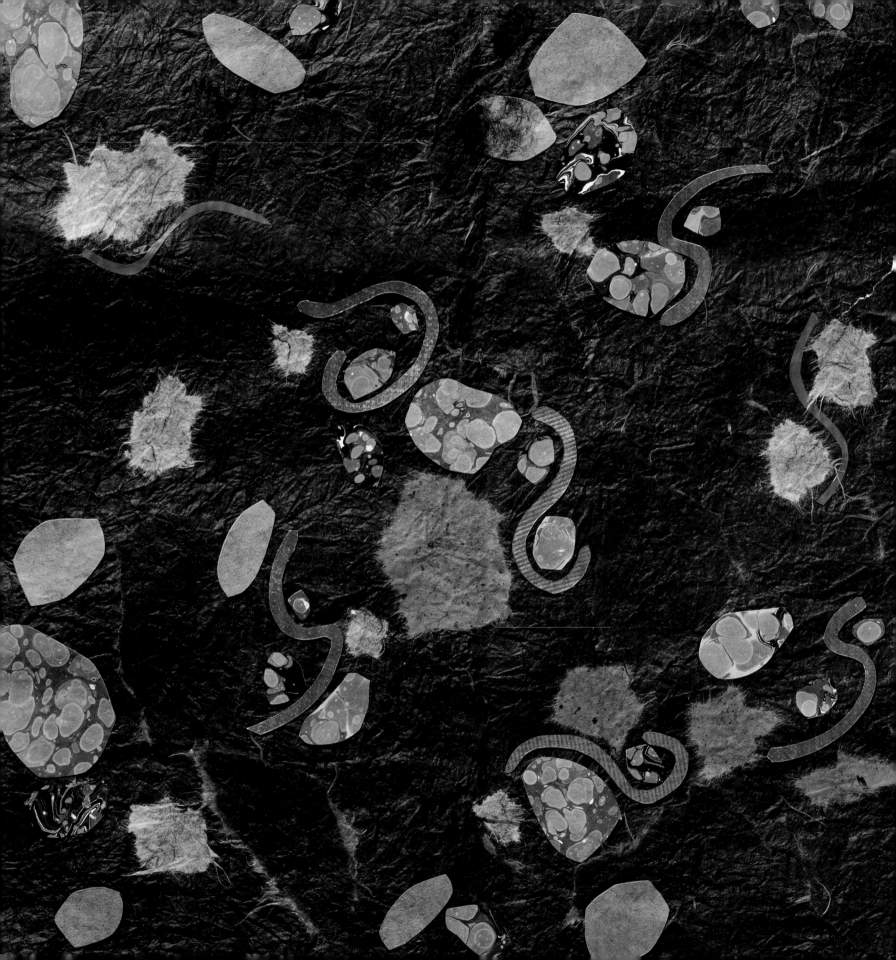

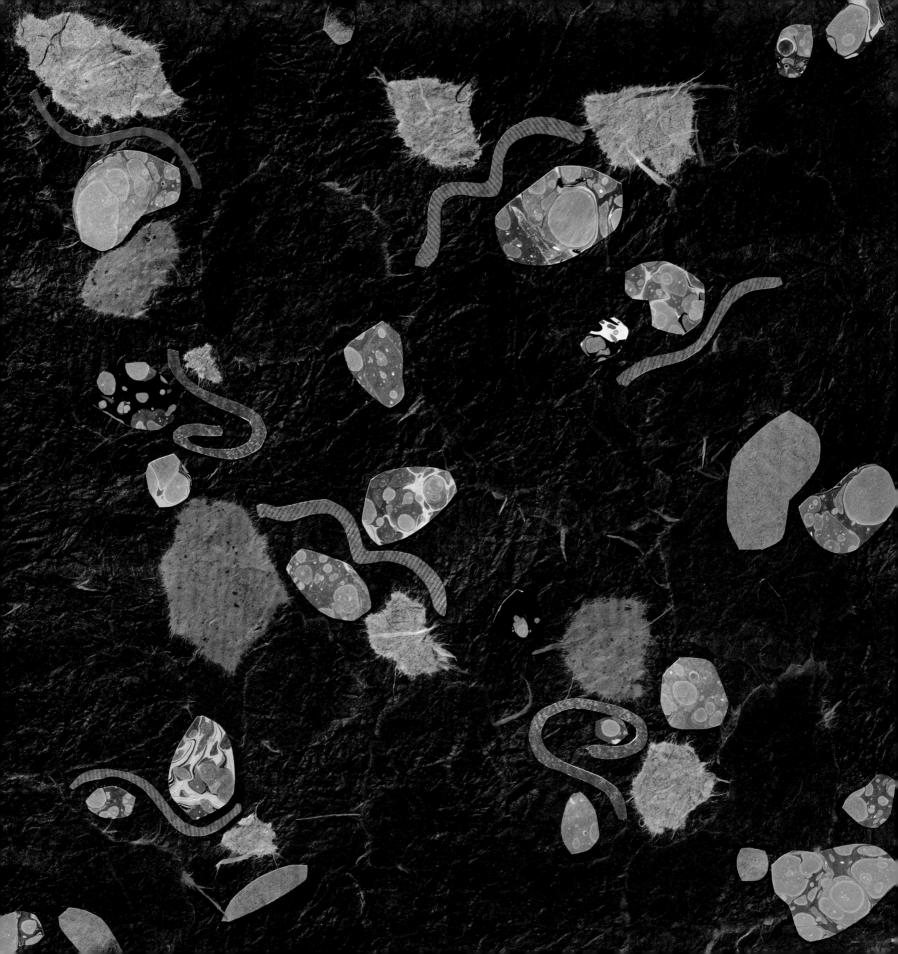

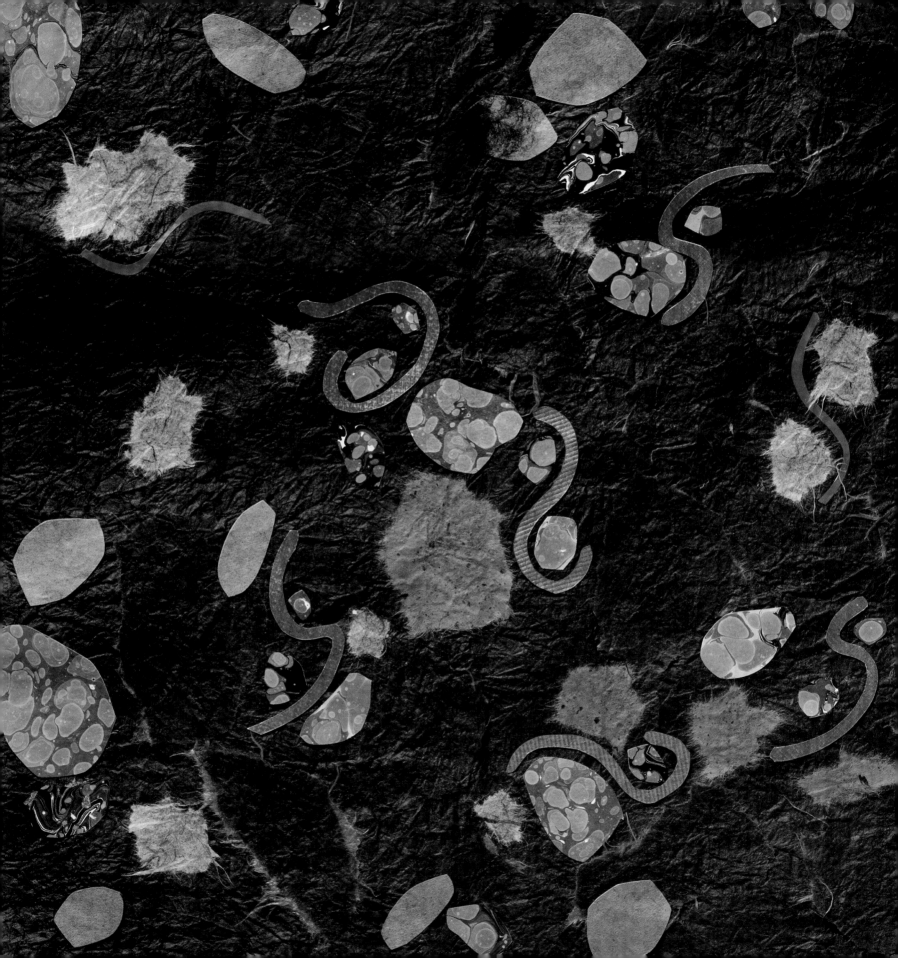

# Compost Stew

## An A to Z Recipe for the Earth

With love and thanks to my mother, who started the first batch,
and to my husband, Owen, who keeps it going.  —MMS

For Nina "MooMoo" Moore, who loved me and her garden,
and for Lucy, who helps me herd all my red wigglers.  —AW

## AUTHOR'S NOTE

Compost is nature's way of recycling. When plants, animals, and minerals break down, they are returned to the earth to become part of the soil. Laundry lint, for example, which is made up of cotton fiber from your clothes, quickly breaks down in the compost. Quarry dust, which is finely ground rock powder, adds minerals that improve the soil. And when worms eat their way through the compost, it comes out the other end as castings that further enrich the soil and help plants to grow. To learn more about composting, visit the Compost Stew page of the author's website at siddals.com/compost-stew.html.

Text copyright © 2010 by Mary McKenna Siddals
Cover art and interior illustrations copyright © 2010 by Ashley Wolff

All rights reserved. Published in the United States by Dragonfly Books, an imprint of Random House Children's Books, a division of Random House LLC, a Penguin Random House Company, New York. Originally published in hardcover in the United States by Tricycle Press, an imprint of Random House Children's Books, New York, in 2010.

Dragonfly Books with the colophon is a registered trademark of Random House LLC.

Visit us on the Web! randomhouse.com/kids

Educators and librarians, for a variety of teaching tools, visit us at RHTeachersLibrarians.com

The Library of Congress has cataloged the hardcover edition of this work as follows:
Siddals, Mary McKenna.
Compost Stew: an A to Z recipe for the earth / by Mary McKenna Siddals ; illustrations by Ashley Wolff — 1st ed.
p.  cm.
Summary: A rhyming recipe explains how to make the dark, crumbly, rich, earth-friendly food called compost.
[1. Stories in rhyme. 2. Compost—Fiction.]  I. Wolff, Ashley, ill. II. Title
PZ8.3.S5715Co 2010  [E]—dc22  2009016300
ISBN 978-1-58246-316-2 (trade) — ISBN 978-1-58246-341-4 (lib. bdg.)
ISBN 978-0-385-75538-2 (pbk.)

MANUFACTURED IN CHINA

13

First Dragonfly Books Edition

# Compost Stew

## An A to Z Recipe for the Earth

By Mary McKenna Siddals

Illustrated by Ashley Wolff

DRAGONFLY BOOKS
New York

Environmental chefs,
here's a recipe for you
to fix from scratch
to mix a batch
of Compost Stew.

Ingredients:

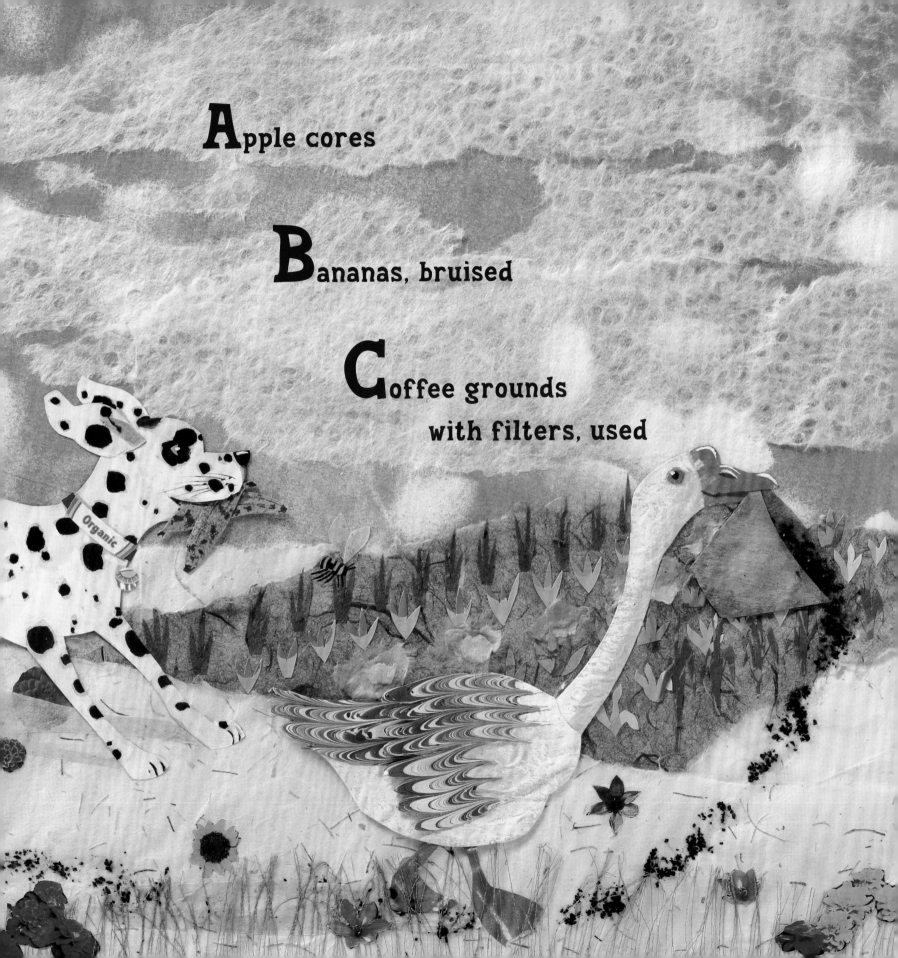

**A**pple cores

**B**ananas, bruised

**C**offee grounds
with filters, used

**D**irt clods, crumbled

**E**ggshells, crushed

**F**ruit pulp left behind, all mushed

**G**rass clippings

**H**air snippings

and an **I**nsect or two

Just add to the pot
and let it all rot
into Compost Stew.

Save: Jack-o'-lanterns

**K**itchen scraps

**L**aundry lint
from dryer traps

**M**ulch removed
from garden beds

**N**utshells

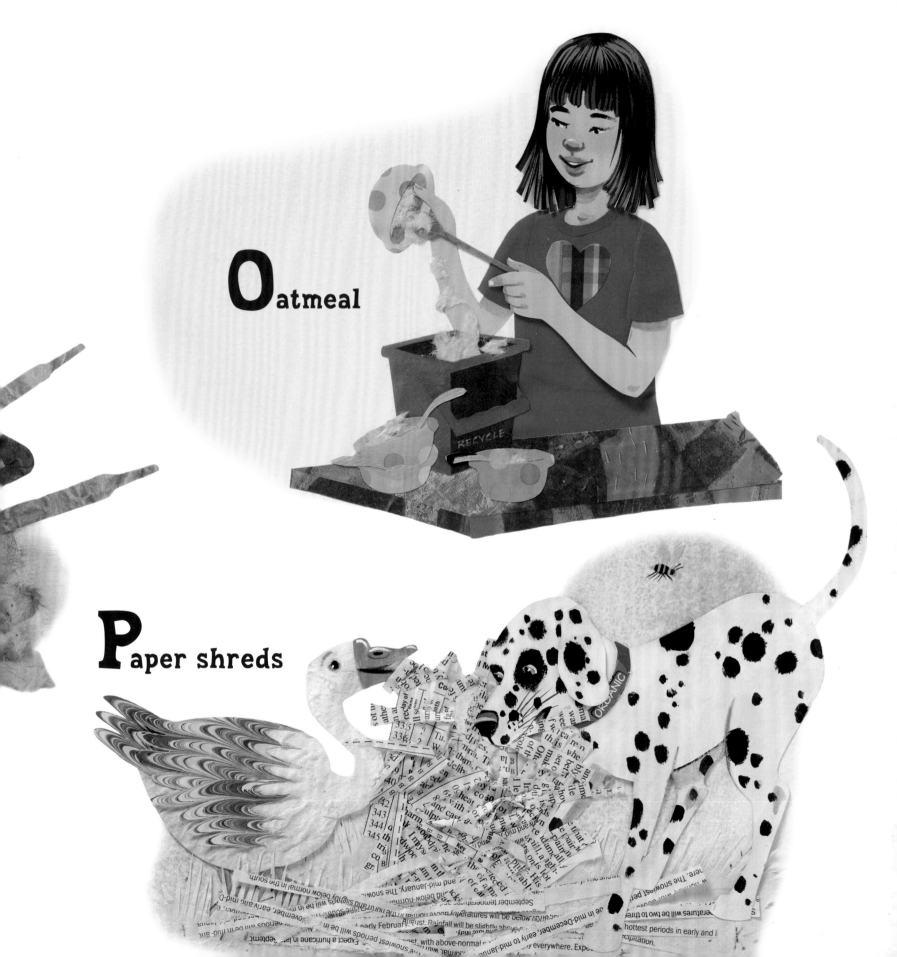

**O**atmeal

**P**aper shreds

**Q**uarry dust

**R**ye bread crust

and **S**eaweed strands
(a few)

Just add to the pot
and let it all rot
into Compost Stew.

**Take:**

**T**eabags plucked from
long, hot swimmings

**U**nderbrush prunings

**V**egetable trimmings

# Wiggly worms with compost cravings

**X**mas tree needles

**Y**ellow pine shavings

and **Z**innia heads
from flower beds
whose blooming days are through

## Just add to the pot
and let it all rot
into Compost Stew.

Cover.
Let brew.

And when the cooking
is complete,
Mother Earth will
have a treat,
dark and crumbly,
rich and sweet . . .

Now open the pot
and what have you got?

Compost Stew!

# Chef's Note

Out of pumpkins? Low on flies? Get creative! Improvise!
You can always substitute any veggie, plant, or fruit.

But please recycle these instead—they won't break down, so not a shred
of metal, plastic, packing foam, or chemicals found in the home.

What's more, no meat or dairy, please. No bones or gravy, fish or cheese,
for these will cause an awful smell, attracting animals as well.

Earthy? Yes! Meaty? No! Synthetic? Stop! Natural? Go!

So spice it up, but be judicious. Keep it wholesome and nutritious.
Mother Earth will say, "Delicious…Compost Stew!"

### Adapting the Recipe for Potluck Contributions
### (or How to Keep Too Many Cooks from Spoiling the Stew):
Ingredients may vary from these general recommendations,
so whenever you've got a community pot, follow your local regulations.

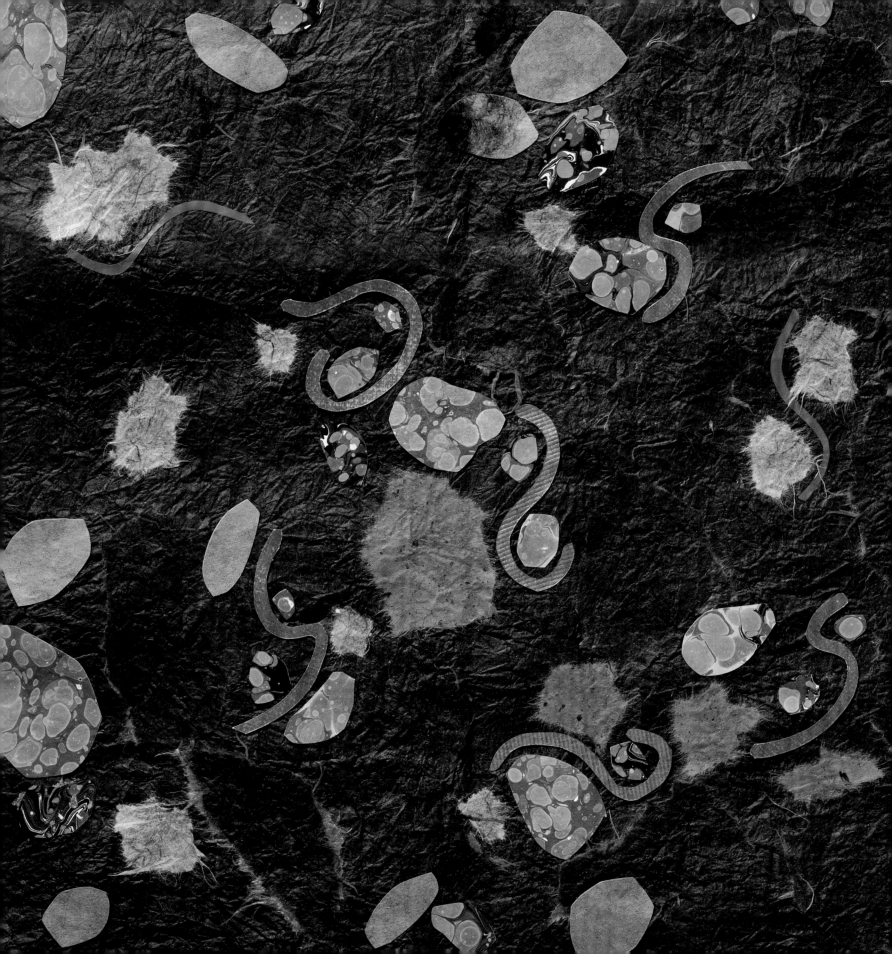

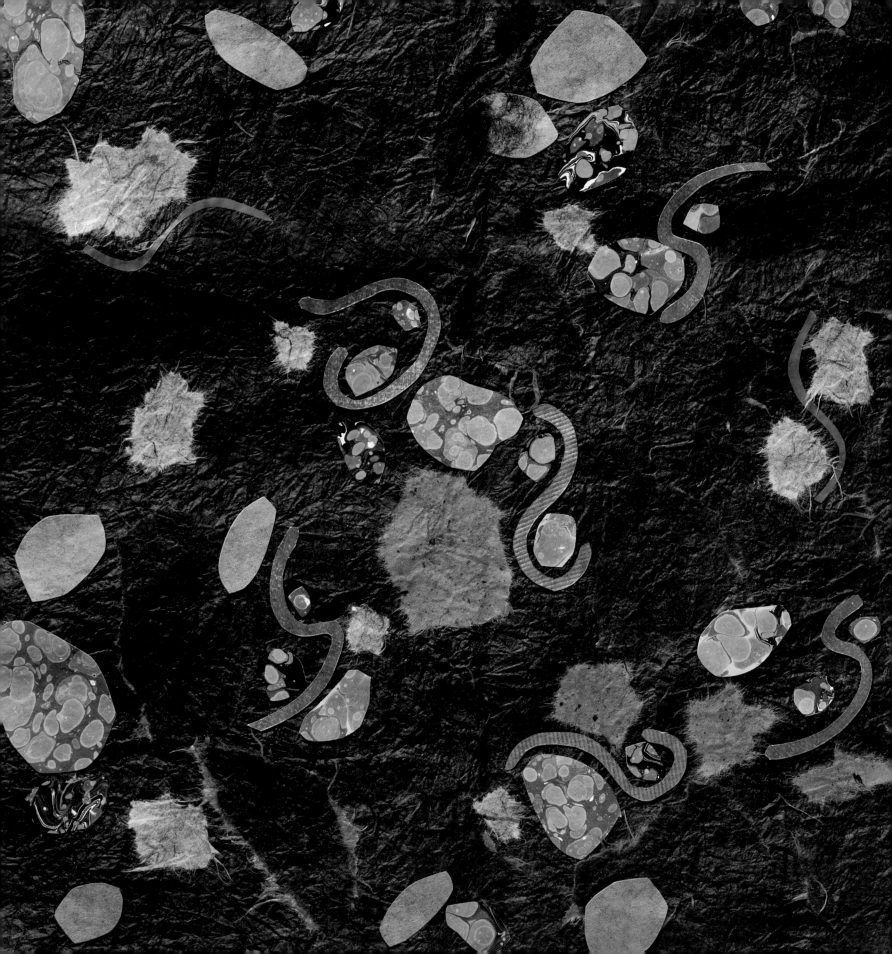

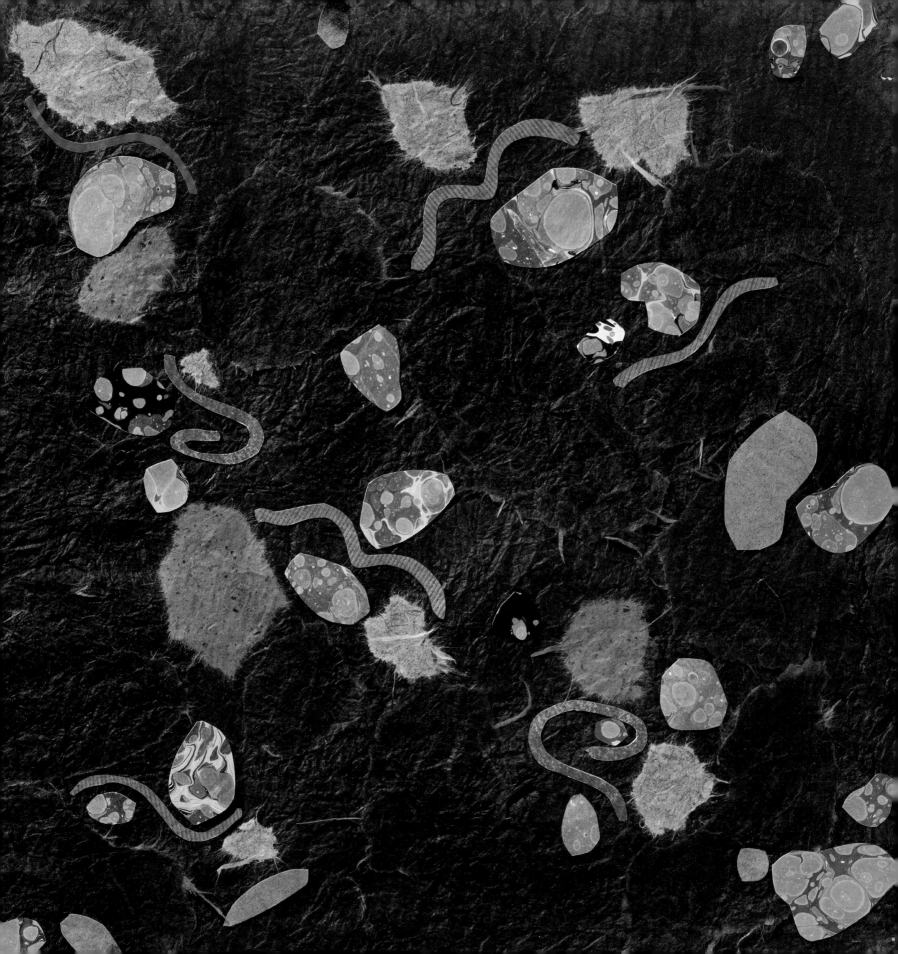

**MARY McKENNA SIDDALS** is the author of several picture books for the very young, including *Millions of Snowflakes*. In addition, she has written dozens of children's stories, articles, poems, and activities appearing in a variety of magazines. A former teacher, she lives in British Columbia, Canada, where she enjoys tending to her own batch of Compost Stew. Learn more about Mary at siddals.com.

**ASHLEY WOLFF** is the author and/or illustrator of more than sixty children's books, including *Baby Beluga*; *I Love My Mommy Because . . .*; *I Love My Daddy Because . . .*; *Mama's Milk*; *Stella and Roy Go Camping*; *I Call My Grandma Nana*; *I Call My Grandpa Papa*; *When Lucy Goes Out Walking*; and the beloved Miss Bindergarten series. Ashley wrangles thousands of red wriggler compost worms in her San Francisco backyard garden. She grows flowers, vegetables, and an amazingly prolific persimmon tree. Visit her website at ashleywolff.com.